REINGO THE GREEN-NOSED REINDEER

WRITTEN BY:
JOHN WESLEY BURTON

REINGO THE GREEN-NOSED REINDEER

WRITTEN BY: JOHN WESLEY BURTON

1st Edition

ISBN: 9798372728769

A Burton Media Group Book
Burton Media Group, Morehead, Ky

Santa Claus

Santa's Elf

It has been a long time since we have heard the story of Rudolph The Red-Nosed Reindeer.

Nobody ever remembered him but Santa Claus didn't forget him. He guided his sleigh though heavy fog around the world to deliver toys to all of the boys and girls on Christmas Eve many years ago.

Rudolph The Red-Nosed Reindeer had a Great Grandson. His name was Reingo The Green-Nosed Reindeer. He had the ability to travel though howling winds.

Santa and all of the elves have been working and toy making throughout the year.

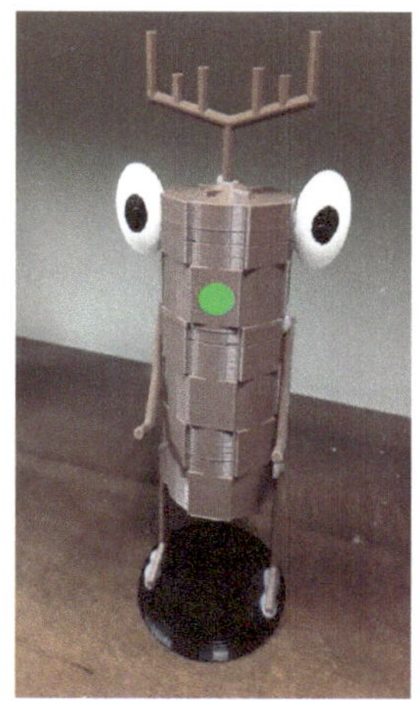
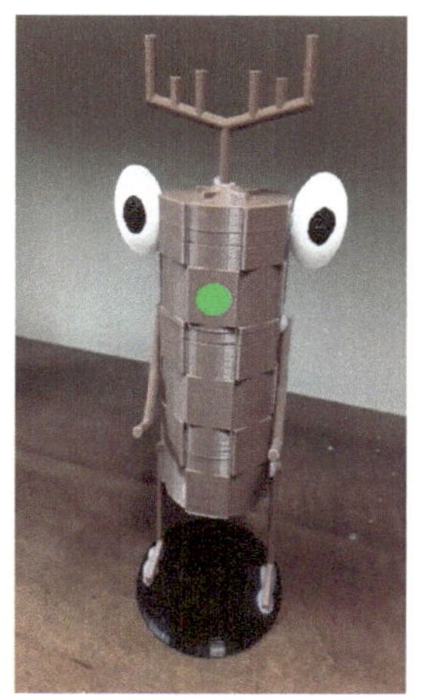
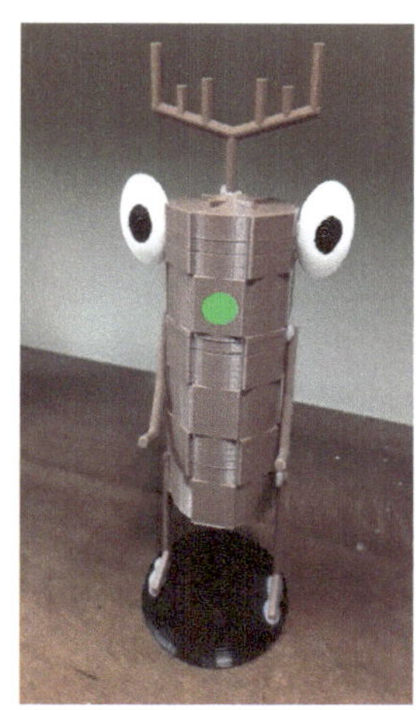

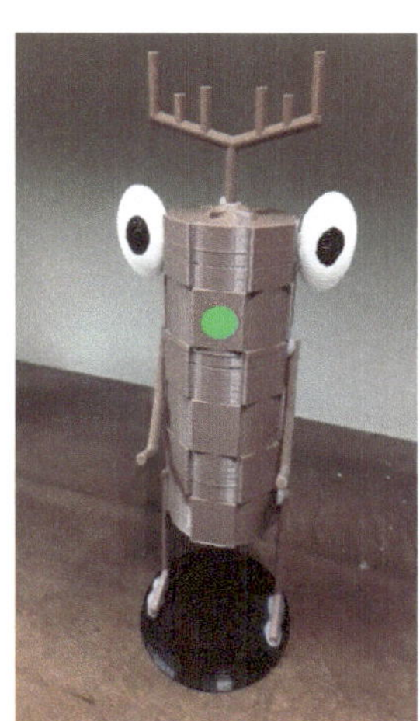

All of the little reindeer seemed to like Reingo The Green-Nosed Reindeer. They let him play some reindeer games with them.

Reingo was a reindeer alright with his green nose that can guide sleighs through howling winds.

The weather was different that Christmas Eve. The winds were forecasted to howl throughout the entire world.

Santa was talking to the little elves at the North Pole on Christmas Eve.

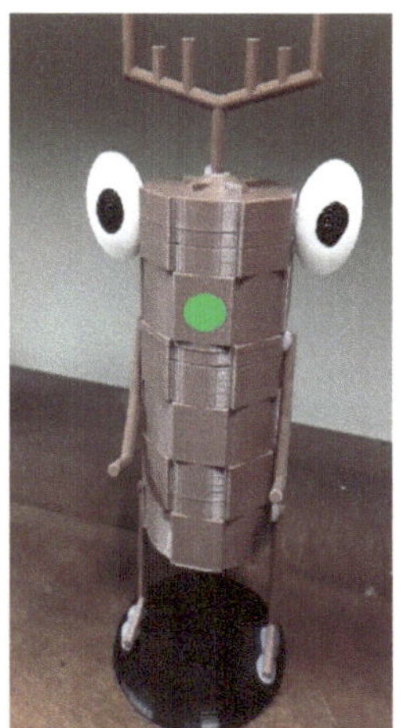

Santa said, "I know of a reindeer his name is Reingo The Green-Nosed Reindeer. He is the Great Grandson of the most famous reindeer of them all. I am going to perform a little magic and ask Reingo to come to the North Pole to guide my sleigh though the howling winds this Christmas eve."

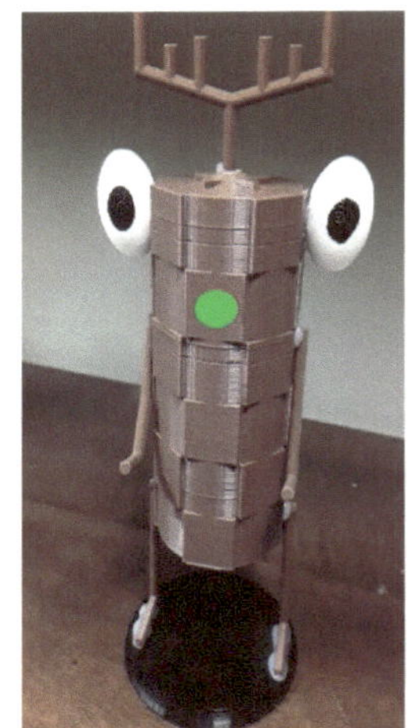

The message traveled from Santa Claus straight to Reingo.

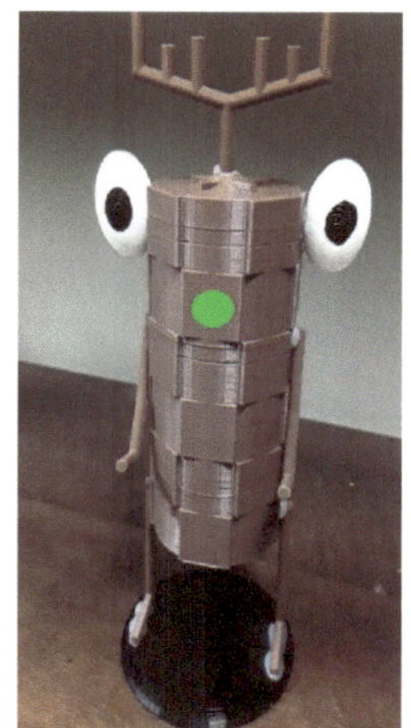

Santa Claus said, “Reingo with your nose so green and having the ability to travel through the winds howling around the world can you guide my sleigh tonight through the winds of everywhere?”

After Reingo received Santa's message, he traveled to the North Pole. He arrived there within a minute's flash.

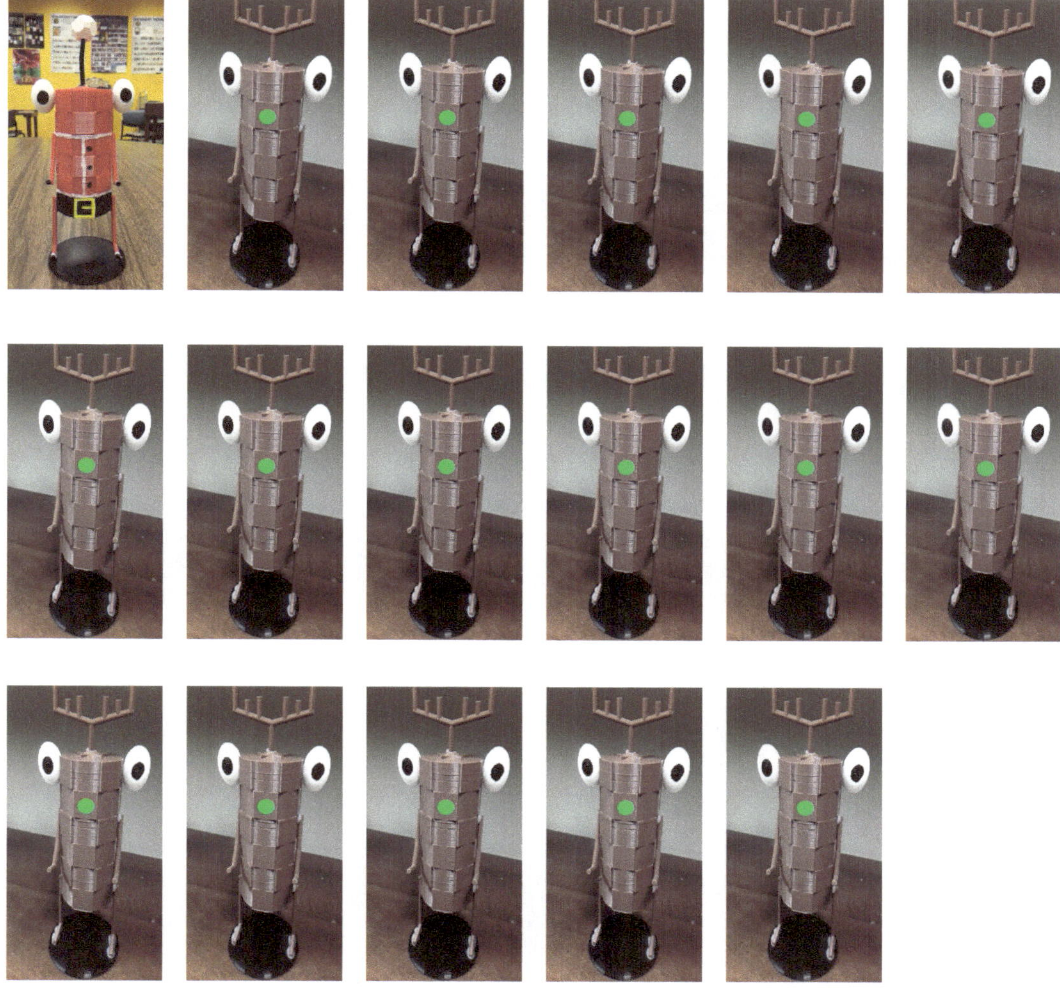

Reingo said, “Santa Claus with my nose so green and my ability to travel through howling winds I will guide your sleigh tonight and the other reindeer and the little elf through the sky this windy Christmas Eve.” There was Santa Claus and the little elf riding in the sleigh and sixteen other reindeer to help guide the sleigh through the howling winds.

Santa’s Sleigh Ride

With Reingo
The Green-Nosed
Reindeer Leading
The Way Through
The Howling
Winds That
Christmas Eve
Was Going Well

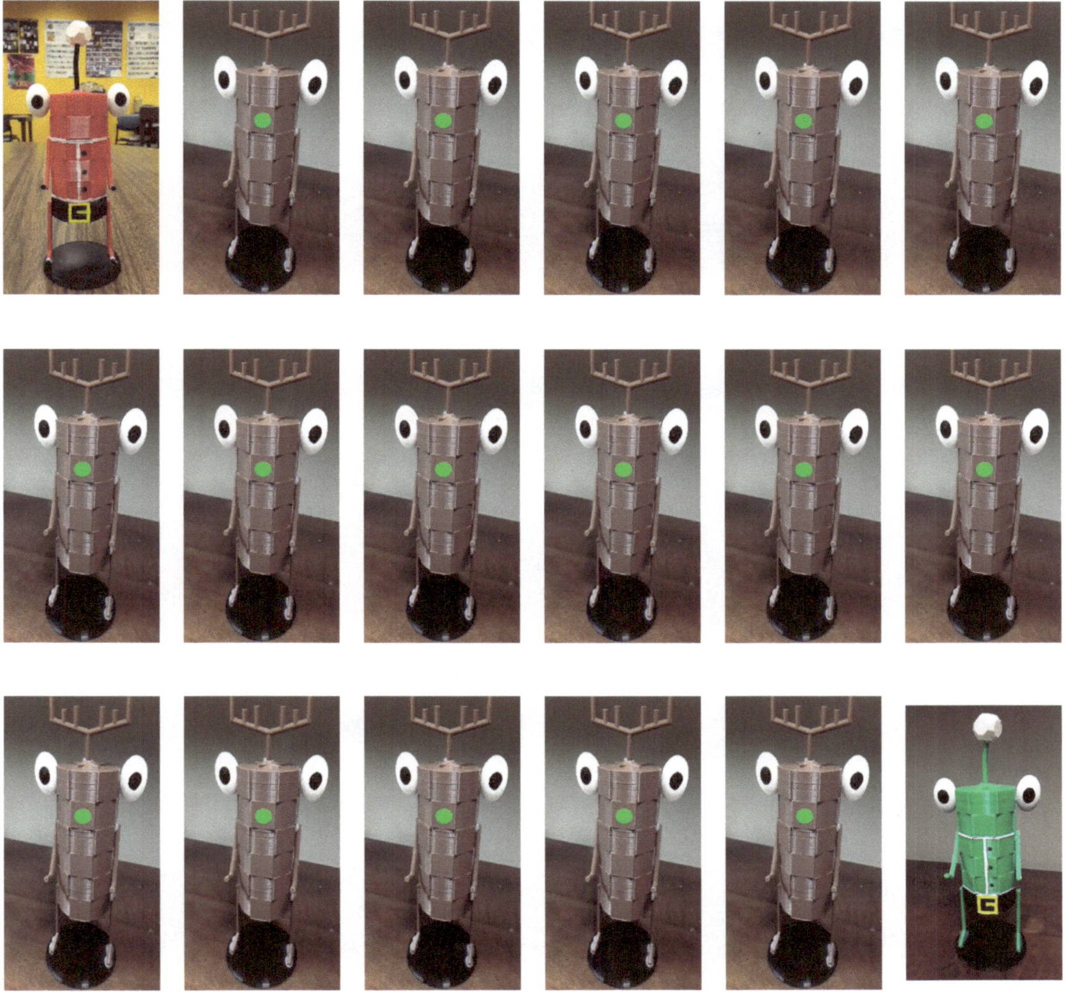

There was Reingo with his green nose so bright guiding Santa Claus, the other Reindeer and the little elf through the howling winds traveling around the world that Christmas Eve.

The toys got delivered to all of the boys and girls throughout the whole wide world.

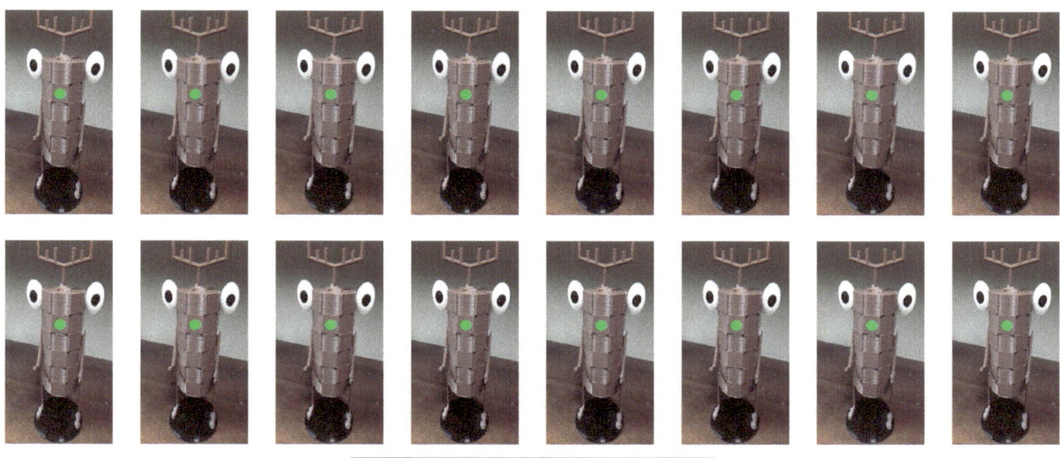

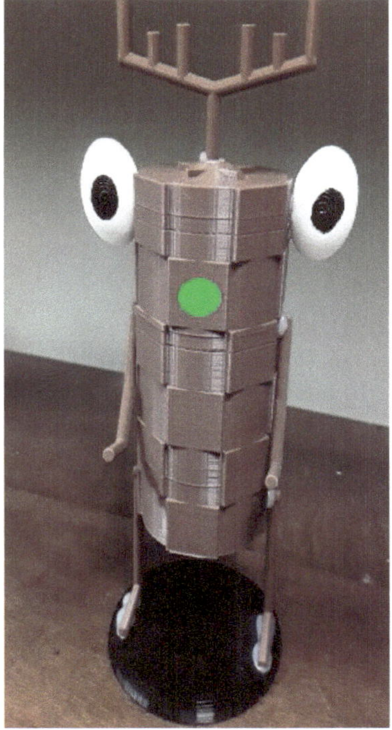

Though out this story the magic of Reingo The Green-Nosed Reindeer has already given the other reindeer a green nose that gave them the power to help guide Santa's sleigh though the howling winds around the world. When the sleigh ride was done the other reindeer had no green nose.

The sixteen reindeer said, "Reingo The Green-Nosed Reindeer

with your nose so green and your traveling through howling winds after guiding Santa's Sleigh with us you will be entered into Santa Claus's Book of Fame along with the greatest reindeer of them all."

Santa Claus

Santa Claus A Next of Kin To Fire Cracker Dan

The original Santa Claus
Was Saint Nicholas
He was a Christian bishop
Who helped the needy
After his death
The legend
Of his gift-giving grew
Saint Nicholas transformed
  into the legendary character
We know today
As Santa Claus
Who delivers Christmas presents
To all of the children
Around the world

Christmas Elf

Santa's Helper
The Elf Another Next of Kin
To Fire Cracker Dan

Christmas Elves tasks
Include making toys
As Christmas gifts
Taking care
Of the reindeer
Baking cookies
Making candy
Preparing Santa's sleigh
And assisting Santa
With other tasks
  One of the primary tasks
Of Christmas Elves
Is the making
Of toys all year long
At the Home
  Of Santa Claus
The North Pole

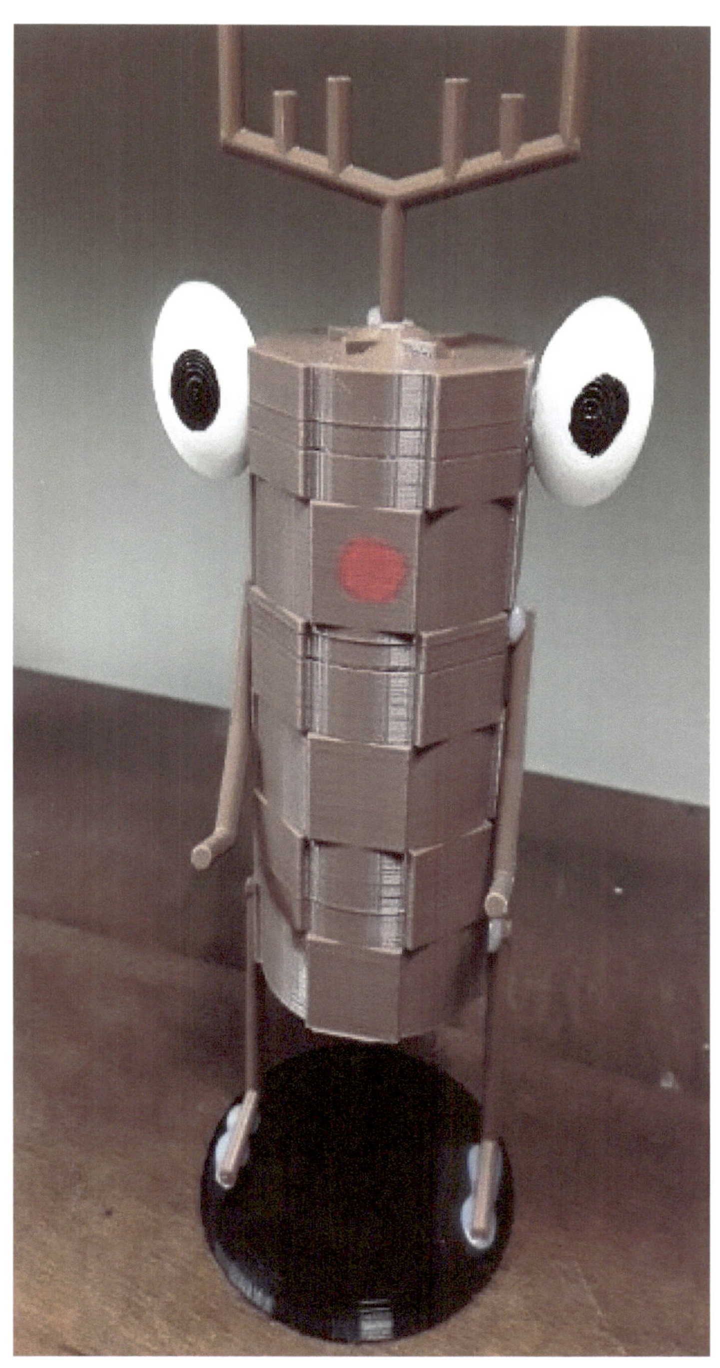

Christmas Reindeer

The Christmas Reindeer
Another Next of Kin
To Fire Cracker Dan

Santa Claus's Reindeer
Dasher, Dancer, Prancer,
Vixen, Comet, Cupid,
Donner and Blitzen
But there's more to the story
Santa's original eight reindeer
Were first introduced
In A Visit from St. Nicholas
More commonly known today
As The Night Before Christmas

Christmas Tree Family

The Christmas Tree Family
Are Next of Kin
To Fire Cracker Dan

Germany is started
The Christmas tree tradition
As we now know it
Sometime in the 16th century
When Christians brought
Decorated trees into their homes
It is believed that Martin Luther
The 16th-century Protestant reformer
Was the first to add lighted candles
to the Christmas Tree

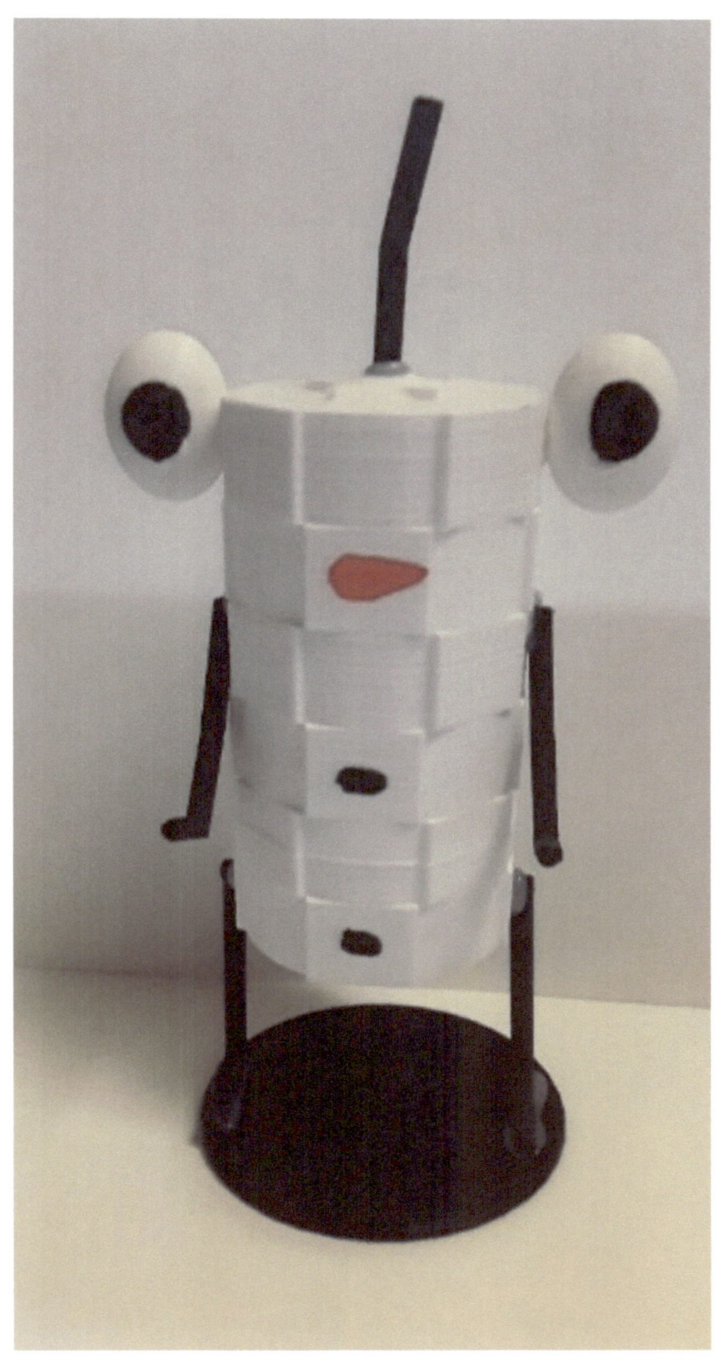

Christmas Snowman

The Snowman
Another Next of Kin
To Fire Cracker Dan

One of the most famous
Christmas animated Television
Christmas specials
Is Frosty the Snowman
It debuted in 1969
Frosty melts
But Santa Claus explains
That Frosty is made
Out of special Christmas snow
And he can never truly melt

Christmas Candy Cane

Candy Cane
Another Next of Kin
To Fire Cracker Dan

The Christmas candy cane
Is a symbol of
The Roots of Christianity
one so old
That we have
All but forgotten its origin
The candy cane takes the shape
Of a shepherd's crook
representing the shepherds
Who were first
To worship the newborn Christ

www.ingramcontent.com/pod-product-compliance
Lightning Source LLC
LaVergne TN
LVHW071215160826
845679LV00003B/836

* 9 7 9 8 3 7 2 7 2 8 7 6 9 *